Eddie and Ellie's Opposites
At the Park

Rebecca Rissman

Raintree

Raintree is an imprint of Capstone Global Library Limited, a company incorporated in England and Wales having its registered office at 7 Pilgrim Street, London, EC4V 6LB – Registered company number: 6695582

www.raintreepublishers.co.uk
myorders@raintreepublishers.co.uk

Text © Capstone Global Library Limited 2014
First published in hardback in 2014
Paperback edition first published in 2015
The moral rights of the proprietor have been asserted.

Edited by Rebecca Rissman, Daniel Nunn, and Catherine Veitch
Designed by Jo Hinton-Malivoire
Original illustrations © Capstone Global Library Ltd 2013
Illustrations by Steve Walker
Picture research by Ruth Blair
Production by Sophia Argyris
Originated by Capstone Global Library Ltd
Printed and bound in China by Leo Paper
Products Ltd

ISBN 978 1 406 26312 1 (hardback)
17 16 15 14 13
10 9 8 7 6 5 4 3 2 1

ISBN 978 1 406 26317 6 (paperback)
18 17 16 15 14
10 9 8 7 6 5 4 3 2 1

British Library Cataloguing in Publication Data
A full catalogue record for this book is available from the British Library.

Acknowledgements
We would like to thank the following for permission to reproduce photographs: Getty Images p. 7b (Howard Denner/Photoshot); Shutterstock pp. 7t (© Ljupco Smokovski), 8, 10 (© 1000 Words), 9tl (© s_oleg), 9tr (© majeczka), 9b (© Juriah Mosin), 11 (© holbox), 12 (© Olena Mykhaylova), 13 (© Paul Maguire), 14 (© tiverylucky), 15 (© amenic181), 16 (© Greenview), 17 (© Zealot), 18 (© Photogrape), 19 (© Darryl Brooks), 20 (© Ohmega1982), 21 (© Margo Harrison), 22, 23l (© yotrak), 23r (© Jaroslaw Grudzinski).

Cover photograph of a playground reproduced with permission of Shutterstock (© kuponjabah).

Every effort has been made to contact copyright holders of any material reproduced in this book. Any omissions will be rectified in subsequent printings if notice is given to the publisher.

Contents

Meet Eddie and Ellie

This is Ellie the Elephant.

This is her friend, Eddie the Elephant.

Ellie and Eddie don't agree on much!

Opposites

Eddie and Ellie like opposite things.

Opposites are completely different from each other.

Ellie likes to listen to **LOUD** music.

Eddie likes to listen to **QUIET** music!

A visit to the park

Eddie and Ellie are visiting a park today.

A park is a great place to spend the afternoon!

Wide or narrow

Ellie likes wide things.
She likes walking on the
WIDE park paths.

Eddie likes narrow things.
He likes walking on
NARROW park paths.

Bright and dull

Ellie likes bright things at the park.
These flowers are **BRIGHT**.

Eddie likes dull things at the park.

These mushrooms are **DULL**.

Big and small

Ellie likes big trees at the park.
This tree is **BIG**.

Eddie likes small trees at the park.

This tree
is SMALL.

High and low

Ellie likes playing on high things at the park. The monkey bars are **HIGH**.

16

Eddie likes playing on low things at the park. The tyre swing is **LOW**.

Fast and slow

Ellie likes going fast at the park.

Riding down the slide is

FAST.

Eddie likes going slow at the park. Climbing the wall is **SLOW**.

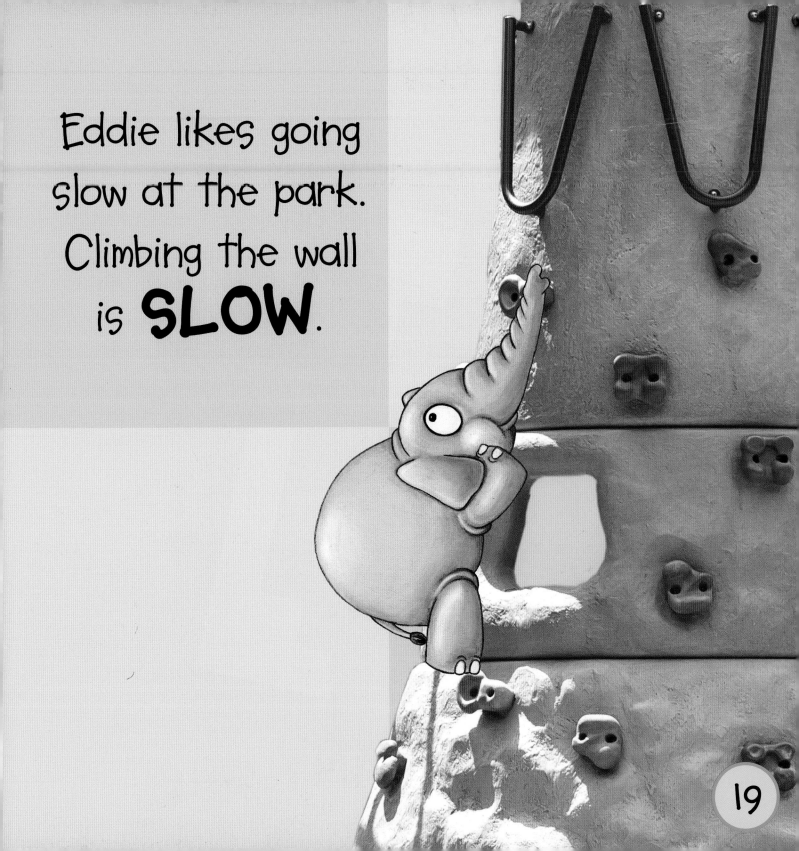

Many and few

Ellie likes choosing between many things at the park.

There are **MANY** swings.

Eddie likes choosing between few things at the park. There are **FEW** see-saws.

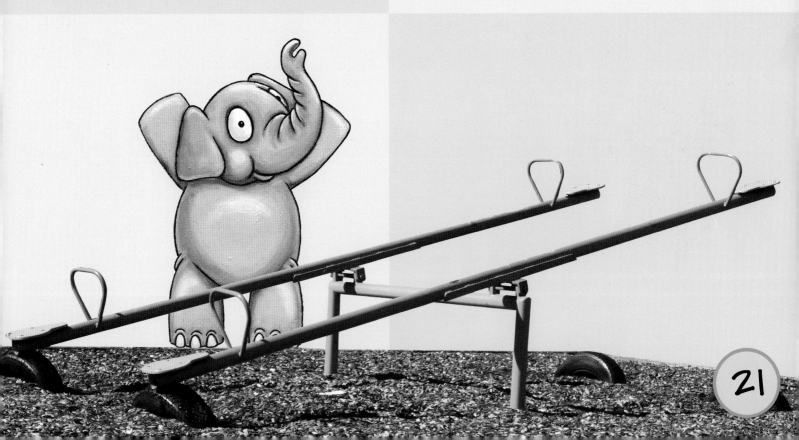

Can you work it out?

Ellie likes playing at the park when it is **HOT** outside.

Do you think Eddie likes playing at the park when it is **HOT** or **COLD**?

Opposites quiz

Do you know the opposites for these words?

young **short** **easy**

Answers

The opposite of easy is hard.
The opposite of short is tall.
The opposite of young is old.
Answers to quiz

Eddie likes playing in the park when it is cold.
Answer to question on page 23